PERSONALIZING JAZZ VOCABULARY

Davy Mooney

To access the online audio go to:

WWW.MELBAY.COM/30786MEB

WWW.MELBAY.COM

CONTENTS

CHAPTER 1

An Introduction to Personalizing Jazz Vocabulary

The Great Disconnect

In my travels as a touring musician and clinician, and as a teacher of applied lessons and graduate level jazz improvisation at the University of North Texas, I have encountered a persistent disconnect that frustrates many jazz students. Most students at the intermediate to advanced level have an impressive command of chord-scale theory, and are skilled at modal and diatonic improvisation. Some of the more advanced students can play highly technical, complicated modern jazz language, but often their playing lacks an essential element: a convincing command of *classic jazz vocabulary*.

When I query students about this, and ascertain that they have transcribed classic jazz solos, I'm at a loss. Why has none of this vocabulary been assimilated, as the chord-scale, modal, and modern information has? Is it that students resist playing material culled from other players' solos? Perhaps, but a more persistent issue is the disconnect between doing the transcription and then integrating and *personalizing* the language of classic jazz into one's own playing.

Some students do this intuitively, and I believe I was one of those. But what exactly does "intuitively" mean in this instance? Surely there was some method that I and others utilized to incorporate this highly sophisticated information into our nascent improvisational voices?

As I began to analyze, retrospectively, what I had done to incorporate and personalize this vocabulary, so that it began to feel like my own, I remembered vividly my first summer jazz camp experiences at Loyola University in New Orleans, in the early 1990s. I was usually placed in an intermediate combo, because I had a ready command of the blues scale, and after a couple of years I learned the modes of the major scale and began to improvise over blues and modal tunes using Dorian, Mixolydian, etc. Around this time, I bought my first classic jazz guitar record, Wes Montgomery's *A Dynamic New Sound*, and I heard it through the filter of my summer jazz camp experience; it sounded like Wes was playing scales, but they sounded more like jazz than the scales I had been playing. I thought to myself, "There must be a *jazz scale* that I just haven't learned yet."

The summer I turned 15, I began to study with the guru of New Orleans jazz guitar, Hank Mackie, and when he realized that I could improvise modally, in the key centers of various jazz tunes like "Lady Bird" and "All the Things You Are," he introduced me to the concept of the *jazz minor* scale.

"Eureka!" I thought, "the jazz scale I've been searching for!" The jazz minor scale, in Hank's nomenclature, was the ascending melodic minor scale, and he taught me that I could play this scale up a half step on a dominant chord that resolved up a perfect fourth or down a perfect fifth, V-I or V-i. Many schools call this scale the super Locrian scale, and I later learned the various modes of melodic and harmonic minor, and harmonic major, etc.

But Hank was wise and experienced enough to impress upon me that the altered dominant sound that the jazz minor scale presented —the ♭9, ♯9, ♭5/♯11, and ♯5/♭13 intervals against the dominant V chord, that had that classic jazz sound that I'd heard in Montgomery's playing—must be treated carefully, and *resolved* to strong chord tones on the downbeat of the measure containing the tonic chord, the I. The strongest resolution notes, Hank taught me, were the 3rd, 5th, and 9th.

He showed me my first ii-V-I lick, and I still remember it:

Ex. 1

This lick (in the style of Barney Kessel and others) incorporates a very common chromatic line over the ii chord, moving by way of a pedal point from D natural downthrough C♯ and C natural to B, the major 3rd (I'll use M3 for major 3rd from now on, for brevity's sake) of the V chord. Jimmy Page uses the same idea in the opening of "Stairway to Heaven." Then on the V chord, the entire *jazz minor* (aka super Locrian) scale is used, incorporating the very dissonant ♯11, ♭13, ♯9, and ♭9 intervals, as well as the more consonant B, G, and F notes—the root, M3, and ♭7 intervals against the G7 chord. **But although the entire scale is used, it is not a random sequence of pitches.** The stepwise resolution to the M3 of the C6, on the downbeat, is essential to the tension and release that makes the dissonant pitches possible, and ultimately quite beautiful.

Licks like this sounded magical to my 15-year-old ears, and *still do.*

Incidentally, I used to think of the I chord in a major key as being a Maj7, but under the influence of Barry Harris and his "6th Diminished Scale" I've begun to think of the I chord as a Maj6. It feels a bit more stable to me, especially on standard tunes from the great American songbook.

One can't expect a student to roll out of bed one day playing, much less improvising, language like example 1. It needs to be played *exactly*, in an exact rhythmic place in the tune, to execute the tension and release and create a sophisticated, beautiful line. I remember soloing on "On Green Dolphin Street" in the key of C my first year at the New Orleans Center for Creative Arts, back in 1995. I would "improvise" on the modal-sounding A sections, and then on the ii-V-I in C that begins the B section I would play Hank's lick exactly. The juxtaposition of my spacey, modal improvising with the language of Barney Kessel was perhaps incongruous, but it made my solo sound more like jazz, *classic jazz.*

Improvising vs. Playing Licks

So, is the solution to the aforementioned "disconnect" to learn hundreds of these lines, and string them together into a sort of pastiche solo? Perhaps. There are definitely great players whose "improvisations" are largely predetermined. In Brad Mehldau's excellent 2003 essay *Ideology, Burgers, and Beer*, he recalls an argument that took place in the late 80s between a group of young musicians over burgers and beers in the West Village of Manhattan. The fight involved the relative greatness of Sonny Stitt vs. Sonny Rollins, the rub being whether it is nobler to aim for a more compositional, *structured sounding* solo (because, of course, composition and structure are always fluid in an improvisation), à la Rollins's greatest work, or a more free-flowing improvisation à la Stitt, who played "great, unadorned bebop," as Mehldau puts it.

Both Stitt and Rollins are great players, and it is silly to pit one against the other (that isn't ultimately the point of Mehldau's essay), but in my own playing and teaching I strive for the Rollins model, ultimately.

My Sonny Rollins was the Joe Pass of the early 1960s, specifically the albums *For Django*, *Joy Spring*, and *Catch Me!* For my PhD dissertation, I transcribed all of Pass's solos on those three records, and tried to analyze and identify what I heard as motivic development—the deep structure (if I can use that loaded term) and apparent formal logic of his improvisations.

I was onto something in that dissertation, although as I look back on my work, the quest was quixotic. I struggled to separate what Pass had improvised, in the sense of *never played before*, from his individual variations on the classic jazz language—those melodic tropes, patterns, and phrases handed down from Louis Armstrong and Sidney Bechet through Hawkins, Eldridge, Webster, Young, Parker, Powell, eventually to Pass, etc. Identifying any essential difference proved elusive.

And so, after transcribing 24 solos, and obsessing over them for two years, I hit upon a concept that I called *question and answer* to describe Pass's method of playing an idea and then answering it logically, through some type of melodic, rhythmic, or harmonic similarity, so that each idea flowed to the next. The end result was a solo that sounded like it had formal, developed motives, almost like a classical composition.

My *question and answer* formulation is similar to Arnold Schoenberg's "developing variation," a concept introduced in the "Criteria for the Evaluation of Music" section of his essay collection *Style and Idea* to contrast the compositional styles of Wagner and Brahms. To read Schoenberg describe it, the Wagner/Brahms dichotomy is remarkably similar to the Stitt/Rollins division that spoiled the burgers and beer session of Mehldau and his buddies:

> *In order to make his [Wagner's] themes suitable for memorability, [he] had to use sequences and semi-sequences, that is, unvaried or slightly varied repetitions differing in nothing essential from their first appearance, except that they are exactly transposed to other degrees...*

Whereas Brahms used:

> *...repeated phrases, motives, and other structural ingredients of themes only in varied forms, if possible in the form of...developing variation.*

Setting aside the whole "motivic development" can of worms, a more interesting question from a pedagogical standpoint might be, "How did Pass personalize the classic jazz vocabulary of his antecedents such that his solos came out sounding original?" Nothing that he plays on *For Django*, *Joy Spring*, and *Catch Me!* had never been played before. Why does it sound like him, while also clearly part of the classic jazz tradition?

Personalizing Jazz Vocabulary

To teach students to personalize jazz vocabulary, as Pass and so many others did, I use a method that is simple in design, but can be difficult to execute. I take a standard jazz tune, a tune that has clear key changes or at least clear tonicizations of closely related keys. I pick four or five measures of the chorus and write out a short passage for the student to play *exactly*, while they improvise everywhere else. The lion's share of these measures are dominant-tonic, V-I or V-i resolution points, so that students are forced to incorporate into their solos altered dominant harmony, chromaticism, and other harmonic and melodic techniques that chord-scale theory doesn't address with enough authenticity to the classic jazz tradition.

On more modern harmonic tunes, I will also write material that attempts to smooth out the dissonant harmony and deceptive resolutions that characterize the work of composers such as Wayne Shorter, Joe Henderson, John Coltrane, and others.

The most important aspect of this method is that it forces students to learn to improvise *into and out of* the written material. I'm not a neuroscientist, but it seems to me that there is a different mental process going on when one plays something exactly than when one improvises. Perhaps the old right-brain/left-brain dichotomy illuminates the difference. I encourage my students to try to *disguise* the written material by improvising something that's intervallicaly, melodically, or rhythmically similar immediately preceding and/or following the written-out part.

To relate the method to my dissertation, the students pose a "question" that is "answered" by the written material, or the material itself is the "question" they must "answer," or some combination of these options. In this way they start a conversation with the classic jazz tradition.

The *Personalizing Jazz Vocabulary* method helps students to assimilate vocabulary into their solos and integrate the improvised and non-improvised mental processes into something more fluid and organic. It also forces them to be aware of exactly where they are in the tune at all times, so that they don't generalize or approximate the form or harmony.

This book presents 10 examples of this method in the following chapters. Each chapter presents one to two choruses (something close to 32 bars) of a chord progression similar to many American songbook and jazz standards. At five points within the chorus(es) a short passage is written out, while the rest of the measures contain slash marks. The student is to improvise over the slash marks and play the written material *exactly*. He/she should also attempt to disguise the written material by improvising *into and/or out of it*, rather than leaving empty space before and after the material. Ultimately, the listener should be unable to identify which material is improvised and which is not.

For each progression, there is audio of me demonstrating the method, along with a backing track for student practice. I also provide an analysis of each written portion. By assimilating, personalizing, and also understanding the theoretical implications of the classic jazz vocabulary, students should eventually be able to improvise with the vocabulary itself, but this is a long-term goal. At the outset, the written material should be played exactly.

What About the Improvised Part?

I have perhaps been flippant in referring to the improvised part of the method. What do students play over the slash marks of these tunes? While it is true that many students who have come up through the chord-scale method of jazz education are skilled at plugging diatonic scales into chord progressions, it is worthwhile to briefly address my thoughts on this topic, although it isn't the focus of this book.

Allow me to digress to the 1966 documentary *The Universal Mind of Bill Evans*, in which the great pianist describes a common issue with intermediate jazz students:

> *I see this in a lot of people who come to me…they tend to approximate the product rather than attacking it in a realistic true way at any elementary level, regardless of how elementary, but it must be entirely true and entirely real and entirely accurate. They would rather approximate the entire problem than to take a small part of it and be real and true about it.*

Evans goes on to demonstrate the issue, on the standard "How About You." He plays eight bars or so in his own style, and then offers an "approximate" version, characterized by harmonic vagueness. Then, to define what he considers to be an "entirely true and entirely real and entirely accurate" form of improvising, he plays simple melodies and arpeggios over the same passage of the tune.

When I teach a class of beginning to intermediate students, I emphasize arpeggios far more than chord-scales. In fact, I present the notes of the full, seven-pitch chord-scale as simply being options to connect the notes of the arpeggio. There are other options as well, chromatic pitches for instance. I often have students arpeggiate chords starting a half-step below the third, rather than the root, so they become accustomed to on-the-beat dissonance:

Ex. 2

In the improvised portions of standard tunes I give students their freedom, but encourage them to arpeggiate chords and to try to hear simple melodies over the changes—and of course to improvise into and out of the written material, something intervallicaly, melodically, or rhythmically similar, to try to disguise it.

That being said, each tune (especially in the case of more modern pieces) presents its own challenges and must to a certain extent be analyzed individually; in this book, I present my method for improvising on each tune at the beginning of the chapter, before analyzing the specific written material.

I also expound on various other aspects of the jazz practice within these chapters, and the organization of these musings may seem somewhat whimsical. I situate these musings as they occur to me, suggested by certain progressions and improvisational situations. They are consistently marked in the text, either by bold font or by a separate heading if the passage is longer than a sentence or two.

Transcriptions and Backing Tracks

For each progression I have included a backing track for you to practice the *Personalizing Jazz Vocabulary* method, with the great Dallas/Fort Worth-based rhythm section of Matt Young (who also engineered) on drums and Mike Luzecky on bass. You can find out more about these great players at mattyoungmusic.com, and facebook.com/Luzecutive.Account, respectively. I provide the comping. We loop through each progression many times, so you can explore different ways to incorporate the written material into your improvisation.

I've also included an example of me demonstrating the method over the same tracks—twice through each collection of vocabulary—and there is a transcription of these improvisations at the end of each chapter. I wanted to be down in the trenches with the readers of this book, and to reveal the results of my own current adventures with the method. Feel free to take anything that I've improvised here and incorporate it into your own playing. Think of it as some extra vocabulary you can use, some *lagniappe*, as we say in New Orleans.

A Note on Fingerings

I've provided fingerings for all the written examples in this book, and they are meant as suggestions, nothing more. I am not entirely systematic about the way I finger things, and I might play some of these examples slightly differently each time. The fingerings I use when I play have been developed over the years through trial and error—with attention to getting as legato a sound as possible, and ease of execution and comfort for the left hand. I try not to stretch when I don't have to. Feel free to adopt these fingerings, or make up your own, but when memorizing new material I suggest you keep your fingerings consistant until you have completely internalized the idea.

Summation

The personalizing jazz vocabulary method is a realistic, thorough, and accurate way for students to incorporate sophisticated harmonic language into their individual improvising voices. I'm reminded again of those jazz summer camps, back in the early 1990s. Even when we were all playing "Sonnymoon for Two," and soloing with the straight blues scale, everyone sounded different. We don't want students to lose that inherent originality, even as they strive to play complex, classic, modern jazz, and learn to speak its intricate language.

CHAPTER 2

Five and Nine Eighth-Note Resolution Cells

When I teach a class of intermediate jazz students, I begin by ascertaining their command of the chord-scales of the tune we are playing. I then encourage them to improvise with more arpeggios, and to start a half-step below the third, as I explained in Chapter 1. As the class progresses, I start to introduce small passages of classic jazz vocabulary. I usually begin with a V-I or V-i resolution, and give students a short, five or nine eighth-note cell to play exactly, while they improvise before and after it.

Why *five* and *nine* eighth-note cells?

In a ii-V-I (I'll use major key Roman numerals for convenience) in which the ii and V chords each occupy a full measure, I give the students eight 8th notes to fill the V chord measure with some combination of chord tones, altered harmony, and chromaticism. The ninth eighth note, on beat one of the I chord, is the resolution. It will always be a strong chord tone of the I chord, and will usually be approached by half or whole-step.

In a ii-V-I in which the ii and V chord are both contained in a single measure, I give students four eighth notes—starting on beat three of the ii-V measure (the beat on which the V chord begins)—that resolve to a fifth eighth note on the downbeat of the I chord measure.

Here are some examples of nine eighth-note resolution cells:

Ex. 3

In this example, the V chord is filled with notes from the B♭ super Locrian scale. The passage begins on the ♯9, and descends stepwise through ♭9, root, ♭7, and ♭13—then skips down to the M3. This skip is very important, and suggests a B♭ augmented triad. G♭ and D are the ♯5 and M3 of this triad, and since the bass is probably playing (or has recently played) B♭, the root, the ear will perceive an augmented sound. The line then continues through the ♯9 and ♭9 intervals to descend to B♭ on the I chord, a very strong resolution to the perfect fifth (I'll use P5 from now on) of E♭6.

Here is another example, in the minor mode:

Ex. 4

The pitches of this cell come from the F harmonic minor scale, a mode sometimes called the Phrygian dominant scale. Again, the most important aspect of this cell is the resolution to the strong minor third (m3) chord tone on beat one of the Fmin. The pitches on the C7 are P5, ♭13, perfect fourth (P4), M3, ♭9, root (R), and ♭7.

Here is one more nine eighth-note example (there are many more in the following chapters), which begins Mixolydian and then turns altered before resolving:

Ex. 5

In this example the only altered note is the ♭9, the D natural on the "and of four," resolving to D♭, the P5 of the I chord. The other notes are from the D♭ Mixolydian scale, although there is a chromatic "enclosure" of the M3 of the D♭7 chord. By enclosure I mean that the targeted note is "enclosed" by pitches a half step above and below—in this case the P4 (G♭) and the chromatic F♭ enclose the F on beat 3. I don't think of that F♭ as a ♯9 in this instance, because it functions as a chromatic passing note. **Chromatic language is an integral part of classic jazz vocabulary, and the universe of chromatic and non-chromatic ornamentation in jazz is every bit as sophisticated as Baroque classical music.**

Here are some five eighth-note resolution cells:

Ex. 6

The four pitches on the D7 chord are a straight D augmented triad, which resolves elegantly to the major ninth (M9 from henceforth) interval of the I chord. Augmented triads are a simple and effective way to give your V-I or V-i resolutions an altered flavor. They can also break up the intervallic monotony of half-step/whole-step lines.

Tritone substitution is another choice of altered language:

Ex. 7

On the G7 chord, the first three pitches are a straight D♭ major triad. The B natural on the "and of four" could be interpreted either as the ♭7 of a D♭7 chord, or as part of a chromatic enclosure of the C natural on beat one of the I chord. **Incidentally, this example is one of few instances where a resolution to the root (R) sounds convincing and appealing. Often, a resolution to the root can be anticlimactic after highly altered or chromatic passages, but here, it works.**

Both the augmented triad and tritone substitution resolutions above can resolve to either major or minor tonic chords, since the resolution notes—M9 and R—don't involve major or minor thirds.

Here is one more five eighth-note resolution cell. This one is taken from that first ii-V-i that Hank Mackie showed me, all those years ago. Taking these five eighth-notes out of that previous context, illustrates how one can eventually free up and improvise with this complex classic jazz vocabulary:

Ex. 8

I have transposed the initial idea up a whole step and made it minor by lowering the resolution a half step to the m3. The pitches on the dominant are the same: ♯9, ♭9, R, and ♭7. This five eighth-note cell is good to have under your fingers, and can help you quickly resolve an (otherwise) improvised line.

Diminished, Augmented, and Tritone Substitution

The examples above present a variety of options for altering and resolving dominants. When I'm improvising a solo on a standard jazz tune rife with ii-V-I progressions, I have a ready collection of classic jazz vocabulary and altered dominant resolutions I can call on. When I'm in the moment, and have to choose how to treat the V-I progressions that come at me in real time, I tend to organize my altered language options into three categories: diminished, augmented, and tritone substitution.

To me, diminished and augmented sounds present two harmonic worlds that have different emotional effects on the listener. The diminished world is characterized by the sound of ♭9 and *natural* 13, whereas the augmented world contains a ♭13. The other altered pitches can be used freely in either of these sounds, but it is really the 13 that determines the augmented or diminished flavor. Example 5 (p. 10) is a straight augmented triad, on the root of the V chord, resolving to the M9 of the I. The only altered pitch is the ♭13 interval, but its presence is overwhelming and places us squarely in an *augmented world*.

Here's a way to treat the Example 6 chord progression with diminished harmony:

Ex. 9

Here, instead of a D augmented triad, resolving to the M9 of the I chord, we have a B major triad (in first inversion) resolving by half-step to the P5 of the I chord. The combination of the ♭9 and natural 13 intervals, the E♭ and B natural, give the passage its diminished flavor. To my ears, the diminished world is more equivocal than the augmented. Diminished chords, and the half-whole diminished scale that composers like Ravel and Stravinsky used to such affect, can be resolved many different ways—there is a fundamental uncertainty to the diminished sound. On the other hand, augmented triads, the hexatonic augmented scale, and the whole tone scale—all sounds characterized by the ♭13 interval—are more emphatic.

This is, of course, subjective, but when I'm improvising in real time, subjectivity is all. I classify sounds this way, and choose which altered world I want to enter based on the effect I want to evoke in the listener.

Tritone substitution, as in example 7 (p. 11), doesn't address the crucial 13 interval, so it is a separate sound to me. Equally affective, in its own way, but more like a hemisphere than a world, if you will.

In the following chapters I will present many more examples of this type of language—augmented, diminished, tritone substitution, as well as chromaticism and other various classic jazz sounds—as five and nine eighth-note resolution cells, as well as in longer and more complex passages. I have also included some tunes with more "modern" jazz harmony—containing progressions that are modal, often with dominant chords that resolve deceptively—to demonstrate how the *Personalizing Jazz Vocabulary* method can work beyond the realm of ii-V-I progressions. Most of this language is in eighth notes, although I have tried to vary the phrasing of the material by starting on different eighth notes of the bar, where feasible.

Keep in mind that the point of this book, and of the *Personalizing Jazz Vocabulary* method, is not only to memorize these examples and get them under your fingers, but to *improvise into and out of them*, so that they can become part of your own soloistic voice.

CHAPTER 3

Happenstance

The chord progression in this chapter is similar to many standard tunes in the jazz repertoire. It is a common jam session progression, and is essential for students to learn if they want to be active, performing jazz musicians. The tune doesn't have any major modulations, but it tonicizes various closely related keys, and there are several ii-V-I/i progressions, as well as the just-as-common IV-iv-I progression that Hank Mackie taught to me as the *subdominant minor cadence*.

I have written out five examples of classic jazz vocabulary in the chorus below, and students should play these examples exactly, while improvising *into and out of them*. Students should also attempt to disguise the written language by improvising something intervalically, melodically, or rhythmically similar leading into and/or out of the given material. The recorded example (the "Mooney Improvisation") contains two choruses where I demonstrate this technique. Again, it is essential that students play the written portion *exactly*, while improvising around it.

Here is a brief analysis of each example, *in the order it occurs in the chorus below*:

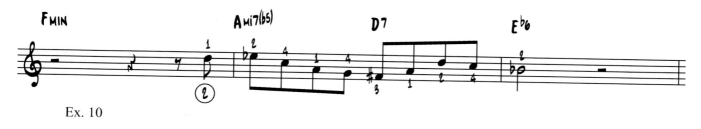

Ex. 10

The chord progression here functions as a minor ii-V-i in the key of Gmin, although the i chord in this instance is actually an E♭6 chord.

In the key of E♭ (and in any major key) the iii chord, Gmin, has a tonic function, and is so similar to the I that the two can be used interchangeably.

In this example the four eighth notes on the Ami7♭5 are largely taken from the chord's arpeggio, although they are presented such that they lead stepwise to the M3 of the D7 on beat three. The D7 is not altered in the sense that was described in Chapter 2. **Instead, this example presents what I call *contouric variety*, while taking its pitches from the arpeggios of the chords. The contour of the line is varied in the sense that the descending first half of the bar contrasts with the ascending second half and, even within those last four eighth notes, the line dips again.** The line resolves stepwise to the strong P5 chord tone of the E♭6.

Ex. 11

This example is more dissonant and altered than example 10. There is a chromatic passing note, an E natural, between the m3 (F) on beat two and the ♭13 (E♭) on beat three. Then a skip down to the M3 of the G7, B natural, evoking an augmented triad, followed by a chromatic enclosure of the resolution note, the P5 (G) natural of the Cmin. The idea begins on beat two and ends on the "and of one" of the Cmin measure. It's important to be able to execute ideas on various parts of the measure, and to sometimes make your resolutions less predictable.

Ex. 12

In example 12, there is contouric variety in the line, as well as a diminished alteration: on beats three and four of the B♭7 measure there is a descending G major triad, with the ♭9 and natural 13 pitches that evoke the diminished sound. This time our idea begins on the "and of one"—a difficult upbeat, but one that we should be able to execute.

Ex. 13

Here is an example that doesn't concern itself with a ii-V-I progression. Instead, we have a scalar passage that contains six of the seven pitches of the E♭ major scale, along with a chromatic passing note, a B natural between the C and B♭ notes on beats two and three of the measure. The idea "resolves" to the ♭7 of the A♭7 chord, as the G natural that is the M3 of the E♭6 becomes G♭, the ♭7 of the A♭7 chord, by way of a diatonic enclosure: G, F, (E♭), G♭. The material over the E♭6 chord could be thought of as a sort of bebop scale, although I must confess I didn't learn my chromaticism through bebop scales.

Ex. 14

This last example is a straight tritone substitution of a G♭ triad against the C7. Once again, we resolve to the P5 of the Fmin chord.

Here is the full chorus, with all the examples in context. Again (not to belabor the point), students should improvise around the examples, but not with them. Listen to the "Mooney Improvisation" for a demonstration.

HAPPENSTANCE

HAPPENSTANCE

(MOONEY IMPROVISATION)

CHAPTER 4

Interstellar

The chord changes in this chapter are an example of a harmonically deceptive progression within a standard tune. I recall spending many hours sitting on a bench outside of my dorm my first semester at the University of North Texas, with my guitar and a metronome, playing these changes over and over, trying to find logical melodies that would navigate their deceptive complexity. **Particularly the first eight bars, which contain a series of deceptive resolutions: Emi7b5-A7 should go to Dmin, but it instead "resolves" to Cmin7-F7—which should of course go to Bb6, but instead moves to Fmin7-Bb7. We don't arrive at the home key of Bb major until bar nine, after a detour to the IV chord, which becomes minor and resolves to I by a more plagal, IV-iv, subdominant minor cadence.** The five examples of jazz vocabulary I have written for this tune attempt to address some of these harmonic puzzles, without eliminating the opportunity for improvisation. Here they are, in the order they occur in the chorus below:

Ex. 15

The language over the A7 chord here is straight D harmonic minor scale, resolving to what might have been the m3 of Dmin, F, but is in fact the P4 of the Cmin7 chord. Somehow it works. Over those hours shredding this tune outside West Hall, I found that both the m3 and P5 of Dmin, F and A, worked just as well as resolution notes on the Cmin7 chord, which allowed me to treat the A7 as still being the dominant of Dmin, rather than having some function in the key of C minor.

Ex. 16

Here is example 6 again, with a chromatic approach, transposed to the key of Dmin. Beats three and four contain a simple, beautiful augmented triad, resolving to the M9 of Dmin.

Ex. 17

This example contains pitches from the G whole-tone scale as well as G super Locrian. However, I would analyze this material as an example of an augmented resolution (containing E♭, the ♭13 interval)—one that initially uses A natural, the M9, before resolving to the P5 of Cmin7 through the ♯9 and ♭9 intervals. The last five pitches are a classic five eighth-note resolution, identical to example 3 from Chapter 2.

Ex. 18

Example 18 contains a tritone substitution on beats three and four of the A7 measure, resolving to the m3 of the Dmi7♭5 chord. One could also conceive of the pitches of the A7 measure as belonging to the A half-whole diminished scale (habitants of a diminished world), but it is the resolution of that scale to the A♭ on beat one of the Dmi7♭5 that makes the dissonant pitches work, regardless of how you contextualize them.

Ex. 19

Here we have a tritone substitution (with a chromatic approach), a B triad over an F7 chord, that resolves to the P5 (F) of the B♭Maj chord by way of a chromatic enclosure.

Here is the full chorus:

INTERSTELLAR

INTERSTELLAR

(MOONEY IMPROVISATION)

CHAPTER 5

Blues

The standard jazz blues progression is of course ubiquitous in the jazz repertoire, and yet it is often taken for granted by intermediate to advanced jazz students. **As a young player, I struggled to achieve what I thought was the correct, authentic amount of "blues" in my "jazz blues." I still work on this aesthetic balance, and make a point to play at least a couple blues tunes on my trio gigs.** The examples below are more concerned with classic jazz vocabulary than blues language, but **two "jazz blues" solos that strike this balance very well, and were very helpful in my development, are Wes Montgomery's "D Natural Blues," from** *The Incredible Jazz Guitar of Wes Montgomery*, **and Grant Green's "Solid," from the album of the same name**. Here are the examples, in the order they occur in the three choruses of B♭ blues below:

Ex. 20

This example addresses the first ii-V-I in the standard jazz blues progression. This line is very direct and simple: the P5 of the Fmi7 is approached from below by a chromatic half-step, and then the pitches are taken from the arpeggios of the Fmi7 and B♭7 chords. The resolution is stepwise, from the ♭9 of the B♭7 to the P5 of the E♭7.

Ex. 21

This example contains a variation on the tritone substitution concept. In this case, both the ii and V chords are substituted for their tritone equivalents: an F♯mi7-B7 progression has been substituted over the Cmi7-F7. Wes Montgomery's compositions often contain this substitution— "West Coast Blues" and "Four on Six" are two notable examples—and Joe Pass's playing is full of these types of lines (as are many other classic jazz solos). **I've always been fascinated by how this harmonic maneuver makes an E natural sound correct against an F7 chord. The M7 interval against a dom7 chord is one of the more dissonant pitches that exists, and yet the structural integrity of the ii-V motion is such that the M7-against-V-chord dissonance is overwhelmed by that E natural's secondary function as the m7 of the F♯mi7 chord that has been substituted.** The resolution is a chromatic approach to the P5 of the B♭7.

Ex. 22

In the jazz blues progression, the sixth bar sometimes contains a passing diminished chord, in this case an E diminished seventh, which functions either as a V of iii or perhaps a V of I six-four, in the classical harmony sense (more on this diminished harmony in Chapter 10). **This line uses the E♭ half-whole diminished scale—which can also be thought of as the four pitches of an E diminished seventh arpeggio, along with the four pitches a half-step below**—and resolves to the M9 of the B♭7 chord through a chromatic enclosure.

Ex. 23

In this example, the progression Cmi7-C♯dim7-Dmin has been substituted over the written ii-V-I in B♭. As with example 21, the results include a M7 interval over the F7 chord. In this instance the pull of the ascending C-C♯-D substitute root movement overwhelms the dissonance. **As a product of jazz education (who very much came up through chord-scale theory), I must confess to a perverse pleasure in making M7s work over dom7 chords.** Something about breaking the rules—I don't know, but resolving to iii instead of I in this context definitely works, to my ears. **But don't take my word for it. Listen to Dexter Gordon's solo break on "You Stepped Out of a Dream" from *A Swingin' Affair* for a classic example of this harmonic maneuver.**

Ex. 24

This last example over the B♭ blues progression is a Dmi7 arpeggio with a chromatic approach to the M3 of the G7, and then a descending D♭ major triad—a tritone substitution—resolving by leap to the P5 of Cmi7. **Sometimes it's nice to resolve more obliquely than the usual half-step or whole-step.**

As I stated at the outset of this chapter, I encourage students to grapple with the right amount of *classic blues language* to apply to *jazz blues*. I haven't addressed that issue here—mainly because it is a large and complex subject, and warrants a book of its own—but it is one we all have to deal with. Again, I encourage students to study solos like the aforementioned Montgomery and Green examples, and to wrestle with this aesthetic dilemma.

BLUES

Blues

(Mooney Improvisation)

CHAPTER 6

Henderson-Type Changes

The harmony of this chapter's chord progression is commonly referred to as more "modern" than the tunes we've looked at so far. By "modern" we generally mean more modal progressions—in this case, major seventh chords move in a whimsical, non-functional way—as well as deceptive resolutions such as this tune's Fmin7♭5-B♭7-EMaj7♯11: a minor ii-V in the key of E♭ minor that resolves instead to an EMaj chord. The material that I have written for two 16-bar choruses of this tune is concerned less with altered dominant, V-I resolutions, as there are fewer to worry about than in Chapters 3 or 4. **The *Personalizing Jazz Vocabulary* method is just as effective for incorporating idiomatic, classic jazz vocabulary on modern tunes as it is on standards.**

Here are the examples from the two choruses of below, in the order they occur:

Ex. 25

One of the challenges of playing Joe Henderson-type progressions similar to "Punjab," "Inner Urge," and "Black Narcissus" is constructing lines that go "over-the-barline." By this I mean avoiding playing an idea on DMaj7, then a separate idea on BMaj7, and a third separate idea on A♭Maj7, etc. Such disjointed improvising can render one's solo monotonous and predictable. In example 25 I have written a line that connects the parallel Maj7 chords "over-the-barline," such that the unusual progression of BMaj7-A♭Maj7—parallel major chords a m3 apart—sounds smooth and logical. The material itself is culled from pentatonic scales. **I like the sound of a minor pentatonic scale off the M3 of a Maj7 chord**—in this instance D♯ minor pentatonic over the BMaj7 and C minor pentatonic over the A♭Maj7.

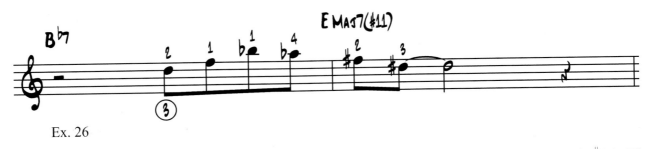

Ex. 26

Example 26 features a straight B♭7 arpeggio resolving to the M9 of the EMaj7♯11. The F♯ and D♯ pitches on the EMaj chord would also work on an E♭min chord. Thus, the deceptive minor ii-V that doesn't resolve to i sounds smoother and more familiar. In fact, the upper structure of an EMaj7♯11 contains an E♭mi7 arpeggio, and **a minor pentatonic scale down a half step from a Maj7♯11 chord (in this case E♭ minor pentatonic) is a common, melodious scale choice.**

Ex. 27

Example 27 connects the parallel Maj7 chords with a line of contouric variety and some subtle chromaticism: the G natural to G♯ that connects the AMaj7 to BMaj7, and the C natural to C♯ that resolves the line. **This example is rather long for our method, but an exception has been made to illustrate how one can counter the rough modal jumps of the harmony with a melodic line that doesn't simply transpose an idea to the various key centers, but weaves skillfully through them.** Schoenberg's Wagner/Brahms dichotomy, from Chapter 1, is perhaps relevant here.

Ex. 28

This line comes from the sixth mode of the harmonic minor scale, often called Lydian ♯2. I like to use this sound over Maj7♯11 chords, to add a touch of mystery to the sound. I was introduced to this harmony by the music of the great New Orleans guitarist and composer Steve Masakowski, who often uses Maj7♯9 chords in his music. The tune "Paladia" from the 1995 Blue Note album *Direct Axecess*, is a good example.

Ex. 29

Here is a ii-V-I that uses the F♯ super Locrian scale to resolve by half-step to the P5 of the BMaj7 chord. There is a chromatic approach to the M9 on beat one of the C♯mi7 chord, but otherwise the material here is scalar—a no-frills, altered dominant ii-V idea.

Page left blank to avoid
awkward page turns.

HENDERSON-TYPE CHANGES

Henderson-type Changes

(Mooney improvisation)

CHAPTER 7

Rhythm Changes

Rhythm Changes is one of the most common chord progressions in the jazz repertoire, and serious jazz students need to be comfortable with it. **With this progression, I still struggle to find the proper balance between "running changes" and improvising.** The A sections of this tune have come to be populated by numerous chords, many more than the original George Gershwin tune "I Got Rhythm," which was basically a three-chord song until the bridge. I tend to want to play all of them—it can become almost a competitive thing, like I have something to prove!

One solution to this problem is to conceive of the first four bars of the tune more like this:

Ex. 30

Rather than this:

Ex. 31

Simplifying the progression, as in example 30, allows one to conceive of the changes in example 31 as *one way* to add complexity to a simple pop song rather than as the starting point of the tune. There's no need to address every chord from example 31 every time—you'll only exhaust yourself, or be transformed into a jazz robot!

For a great example of true *improvising* over Rhythm Changes, listen to John Scofield's masterful "Wee," from the album *En Route*.

Here's an example of thinking of the simpler example 30 chords over the I-VI-ii-V pattern that the rhythm section will undoubtedly play behind your solo. This is the first example from the chorus below:

Ex. 32

The language here is not concerned with the G7-Cmi7 portion of the progression. Instead, the harmony is B♭ major, with a chromatic G♭ passing note between the G and F, and a fragment

34

of an augmented triad over the F7 to resolve to the M9 of a B♭Maj chord instead of the written Dmi7.

By way of contrast, being able to "run changes" like this next example is definitely useful, and I can call on this type of language in a pinch:

Ex. 33

But the challenge of Rhythm Changes to me is improvising, not running changes.

Licks vs. Tropes

One more point, and perhaps a slight digression, about example 33 above. It contains great, classic jazz vocabulary, but I haven't included it in the written chorus because a line this long and complex isn't as conducive to the *Personalizing Jazz Vocabulary* method as the shorter, simpler "tropes" that I've included. I must credit the great guitarist Brad Shepik, and his excellent improvisation class at New York University, with the jazz "trope" concept I've just mentioned. A jazz "trope" is a fragment of the jazz language, a short idea that one hears over and over again, with slight rhythmic and melodic variations, like the examples I've been writing in this book—many of which are similar. On the other hand, example 33 above is more of a "lick:" a series of tropes strung together in a particular order. The ultimate goal of the *Personalizing Jazz Vocabulary* method is to learn enough of these tropes so that you can eventually improvise with them, and string them together into complex passages of your own.

Ex. 34

Example 34 is similar to example 23 from Chapter 5. Again, we are basically ignoring the written F7-B♭6 progression and substituting A7-Dmin, a V of iii in the key of B♭. The pitches over the F7 chord are taken from an A7 arpeggio, with a chromatic approach from D♯ to E natural, and eventually resolving to the m3 (F) of the substituted Dmin chord, which is also the P5 of the written B♭6. **Again we see that on Rhythm Changes, blues, and many standard tunes, one can substitute various progressions on top of what is written, provided there is a strong sense of tension and release.**

35

Ex. 35

This example addresses the second half of the A section, which tonicizes the IV chord, and returns to I either through a subdominant minor iv-I progression, or a ♯iv diminished-I. In this case, the language is straight E♭ major scale, with the G natural lowered to G♭ to reflect the m3 of the E♭mi6 chord. **This line is simple, but has an appealing, over-the-barline feel.**

Ex. 36

Here we have an Amin9 arpeggio—closely related to the written D7—which is altered on beat four with a ♭13, evoking an augmented sound as it resolves through the M3 of D7 to the M9 of G7.

Ex. 37

This line is a tritone substitution of a B13 sound over the F7, resolving to the P5 of the B♭6 chord. The initial descending P4 interval is a nice contour shift, although it is followed by minor thirds, half-steps, and whole-steps.

As with blues, I force myself to play Rhythm Changes on my trio gigs, and I strive for a mixture of "running changes" (with material like example 33) and improvising over simplified harmony. I use the tropes of the jazz language that I have personalized over the years, so that I don't feel shackled to the endless I-VI-ii-V cycles.

RHYTHM CHANGES

(MOONEY IMPROVISATION)

CHAPTER 8

Coltrane-Type Changes

Negative Guide Tones

Another progression that is difficult to improvise on, rather than just run changes, is the harmonic cycle that John Coltrane used to great effect in "Giant Steps," "Satellite," "Countdown," and many other compositions and arrangements. One method that I employ to play on this tune, outside of the *Personalizing Jazz Vocabulary* method, is to search for what I call "negative guide tones." Guide tones commonly refer to the thirds and sevenths of chords, which are pitches that usually change from chord to chord, so that one can clearly perceive the movement of the harmony. Negative guide tones, on the other hand, are notes that stay the same from chord to chord. On tunes that employ the Coltrane cycle the changes move rapidly, jumping in major and minor thirds. Having some common tones or negative guide tones to construct your lines around can help smooth these large leaps. Here is an example:

Ex. 38

In this case I'm using the notes D and D♯ as negative guide tones to connect this line through the changes. D is the P5 of G6, the M3 of B♭7, the major seventh (M7) of E♭6, and later the root of D7, while D♯ is the major sixth (M6) of F♯7 and the M3 of B6.

Here is another example:

Ex. 39

In this case F♯ and G are the negative guide tones.

Please excuse that brief but necessary digression from the *Personalizing Jazz Vocabulary* method. The peculiarity and complexity of Coltrane harmony requires some explanation beyond providing five examples of vocabulary. Here is a brief analysis of each example from the two choruses below, in order of occurrence:

Ex. 40

The pitches here mix scalar material from D Mixolydian with arpeggios over the G6 and the B♭7. The G natural on the "and of two" in the second measure almost feels like a chromatic passing note to the A♭ on beat three, although it is of course the root of the G6 chord.

Unusually, I haven't used any altered dominant harmony here, and I haven't resolved on beat one of the E♭6 measure (not shown here). Or at least I've resolved early, since the B♭ on the "and of four" is the P5 of the E♭6. **I find that during measures 1-2 and 5-6 of this progression, it isn't necessary to alter the dominants. There isn't enough time, really, and the chords jump around so much that more consonant resolutions sound sophisticated on their own.**

Ex. 41

One can't get simpler than example 41: an F♯7 arpeggio (first inversion) resolving step-wise to the M3 of B6. **As I stated above, simple, consonant resolutions like this are enough, especially during measures 1-2 and 5-6.**

Ex. 42

Here we have an arpeggio on the Fmi7, followed by some altered harmony on the B♭7: a descending B minor triad, a dissonant upper structure. The resolution is a chromatic enclosure of the P5 of the E♭6, B♭, on the customary first beat of the measure.

Ex. 43

The longer example 43 contains language that combines scale fragments, arpeggios, and two resolutions by chromatic enclosure: the first encloses the P5 (B♭) of the E♭6, the second the M7 A♯ of the B6.

Ex. 44

In this example, the C♯mi7 is treated with a simple, root position arpeggio. The F♯7 line contains an interesting combination of pitches: the M3, followed by the M9 and the ♭9, and then a resolution to the P5 of the B6 through the M6 of the F♯7. **I'm not familiar with a chord-scale that combines this particular group of altered and consonant pitches.**

I classify "Coltrane Changes" and "Rhythm Changes" similarly, as progressions that are difficult to improvise and play melodically on, rather than simply (although of course it is anything but simple!) running changes. The *Personalizing Jazz Vocabulary* method has helped me and my students square the circle, even as these progressions present an enduring challenge.

Coltrane-type Changes

(Mooney Improvisation)

CHAPTER 9

Golson-Type Changes

This chapter's progression is similar to the work of Benny Golson, another harmonically sophisticated modern jazz composer. There are aspects of the harmony explored here that I treat similarly to Coltrane changes. During the A sections of this progression, ii-V progressions rise and fall by half-step, only resolving to I at the end of measures four and twelve. To avoid the Wagnerian trap (if you will) of playing an idea and then transposing it up a half-step, ad nauseum, I use the same *negative guide tone* concept that helps me through Coltrane changes:

Ex. 45

In the first two bars of this example, I'm using the note D♭/C♯ as a pivot, or negative guide tone, between B♭min7 and Bmin7. D♭ is the m3 of the B♭min7 chord, while its enharmonic equivalent, C♯, is the M9 of the Bmin7.

The negative guide tone concept is related to what Jerome Kern labeled *enharmonic modulation*. Kern uses the technique at the end of the bridge of "All the Things You Are," where a G♯ on an EMaj chord, a M3, becomes an A♭ on a C7, the ♭13, to modulate from E major to F minor. Coltrane's "Moment's Notice" also uses this technique.

In bars three and four above, a negative guide tone A♭, the m7 of the B♭min7 chord, becomes G♯, a M6 on the Bmin7. **These two lines don't have the stock feel of an idea played and then transposed up a half-step. That being said, Lee Morgan's exquisite solo on the original recording of this tune does just that—sometimes things are "stocked" for good reason.**

Example 45 is too long for the *Personalizing Jazz Vocabulary* method, although I have used a fragment of it below. Here are the examples from the chorus below:

Ex. 46

Measures five through eight of this progression contain a descending progression: A6-A♭7-G6-G♭7. One can treat the dominants here with a variety of jazz language. In this case I have used augmented harmony on the A♭7, with a half-step approach to the M3, B to C. This chromaticism gives the line a hexatonic, augmented scale feel, although it omits two of the six pitches of that scale. The resolution to the M7 of the G6 chord is pleasantly unpredictable.

Ex. 47

Here is a classic example of a nine eighth-note resolution cell. The pitches on the Gmin7 are from its arpeggio, while the C7 contains ♭9, M3, and a chromatic enclosure of the resolution note, the M3 (A) of the F6.

Ex. 48

Example 48 is another nine eighth-note resolution cell, its language culled from the G harmonic minor scale, with a chromatic passing note D♭ between D and C on the Ami7♭5. The pitches on the D7 contain a ♭9 (E♭), resolving by half-step to the P5 (D) of the Gmin chord.

Ex. 49

Example 49 is a fragment of example 45 above. **The A♭/G♯ enharmonic suggests oblique motion between bass and melody.**

Ex. 50

Over measures 29-33 of this progression, Cmi7♭5-F7-B♭mi7♭5-E♭7-A♭6, I find that melodic minor harmony works very well. **On the mi7♭5 chords I play a melodic minor scale up a minor third, and on the dominant chords a melodic minor scale up a half-step—the famed**

super Locrian scale. It seems to me to be the right treatment of this harmony, although there are many other valid options, of course. In this example I haven't resolved to the B♭min7♭5 chord. This is mostly for variety's sake. I could have written a line like this, with some chromaticism and a resolution to the m3 of the B♭min7♭5:

Ex. 51

Benny Golson's harmony is a specific area of study for me and my students. He is one of the major jazz composers, along with Coltrane, Monk, Shorter, Silver, and a few others. "Stablemates," "Along Came Betty," "Whisper Not," "Killer Joe"—all classics. The *Personalizing Jazz Vocabulary* method can help students navigate the tricky harmonic puzzles that Golson constructs.

GOLSON-TYPE CHANGES

Golson-type Changes

(Mooney Improvisation)

CHAPTER 10

No One

Returning to a standard progression, albeit a complex one, this chapter's changes are a tour de force of subtle, unpredictable modulation. There are also interesting uses of diminished chords, especially in bars 10 and 32.

The diminished progressions offered here are interesting to me, because they resolve deceptively. In measures 9-11, the chords are E6-E♯dim7-B/F♯. We would normally expect the E♯dim7 to resolve to an F♯ chord of some sort, probably F♯min. However, although there is an F♯ in the bass of the BMaj chord, and we could conceive of this resolution as being IV-♯ivdim-I⁶, I consider the function of this diminished to be V of iii or iii⁶ in the key of BMaj. **The E♯dim7 can be thought of as A♯7♭9/E♯, a dominant seventh with the fifth in the bass, which resolves to D♯min (with F♯ in the bass), the tonic functioning iii chord in the key of B major.**

In measures 31-33, we have Dmin-E♭dim7-Dmin. We would expect the E♭dim7 chord to move to C/E, or Emi7, like the substitution we explored in example 33 from Chapter 7. But the changes defy our expectations and the E♭dim7 "resolves" back down to the Dmin chord from whence it came.

Here are the examples from the chorus below, which address these deceptive diminished resolutions, as well as other progressions:

Ex. 52

The first harmonic "trick" in this tune is a rapid-fire modulation from C major to B major. After four bars of common C major harmony, there is a ii-V in C, and then with no warning, a ii-V to B. The line in example 52 is an over-the-barline attempt to smooth out this jagged, abrupt modulation. There is a chromatic B♯ over the C♯min chord, which briefly tonicizes C♯ minor, but otherwise the pitches are all from their respective chord-scales and arpeggios.

Ex. 53

Example 53 contains that first, deceptive use of a diminished chord that we discussed above. Since the Fdim7 (E♯dim7, technically) is resolving to the iii chord in the key of B major, the pitches I have chosen are from the E♭/D♯ harmonic minor scale—more specifically a B♭7/A♯7 arpeggio, with a chromatic passing note between B♭ and A♭, resolving to the P5 F♯ of the B/F♯ chord.

Ex. 54

Here is one of our customary nine eighth-note resolution cells. **This material is an effective use of upper structure triads, similar to example 42, from Chapter 8. In this case, a Bmin arpeggio over the Emi7 chord descends to a B♭min arpeggio over the A7, resolving with a chromatic enclosure of the P5 (A) of the Dmi7.**

Ex. 55

This progression is a iv-I resolution, a subdominant minor cadence, with the iii chord Emi7 substituted for the I, which would have been CMaj. **Minor iv to I is a very common progression in standards—second only, perhaps, to the ii-V-I.** The pitches are straight from the major mode chord-scales, with some contouric variety added to the line.

Ex. 56

In this example, we explore the second of the aforementioned, deceptive diminished resolutions. **Even though this E♭dim7 doesn't resolve to Emin or C/E, I still treat it as a B7♭9 chord, and the pitches I have chosen are from that arpeggio, with some chromaticism and a resolution by leap, from B to the m3 (F) of the Dmi7.**

No one

No One

(Mooney Improvisation)

CHAPTER 11

Monk-Type Changes

Thelonious Monk is a canonical jazz composer, and the chord changes in this chapter are a good example of his approach to harmony. They contain some quick modulations, and dominant cycles that move at the harmonic rhythm of one chord per beat. **It can be tempting to either approximate or skip over these harmonically "busy" sections of the tune, but I would draw your attention to Lucky Thompson's solo on the 1952 recording of Monk's "Skippy," Sonny Rollins solo on the original take of "Pannonica," and Johnny Griffin's solo on "Light Blue," from the 1958 album "Thelonious in Action," as three examples of tenor saxophonists who play *all* of Monk's changes. Coltrane is of course another example.**

There is a tendency toward, for lack of a better term, "quirky" affectations when playing Monk's music, especially with younger, less experienced players. But when one studies the original recordings of his oeuvre, it is clear that the musicians therein *accurately* execute the intricacies of his harmonies. They really get inside of his music, rather than scratching the surface or (to use Bill Evans's term) *approximating* it with self-conscious dissonance and weirdness. The five examples below can help students in this regard.

Ex. 57

Over many years of playing these changes, I have discovered that a fully altered Bb7 isn't the most effective option over this tonicization of Eb major, at least from my aesthetic perspective. In example 57, I stick to a Bb7 arpeggio, with a chromatic enclosure of the M3 of the Eb6 chord. I have also anticipated the Bb7 by an eighth note. With tunes that modulate at this harmonic rhythm, it is okay to anticipate the harmonies a bit—this is the converse of over-the-barline phrasing, and can add depth to one's improvising if not overdone.

Ex. 58

Given that this chord progression is often played as a ballad, it is helpful to have some sixteenth-note language. In example 58, we still have a nine eighth-note resolution cell, but it occupies two beats instead of four. This is a deceptive chord progression; it feels like it wants to resolve to C major, even though there is a ii-V in Db in the first part of the measure. Luckily, the note G is the P5 of CMaj as well as the #11 of DbMaj7, and we can play off of that dual function to embrace the ambiguity of the progression. The language over the Ab7 is chromatic, sort of a fragment of a bebop scale. The C on beat four of the measure functions as the M3 of the Ab7 chord as well as part of a chromatic enclosure of the M3 (B) of the G7. We resolve smoothly to the #11 (G) by half step.

Ex. 59

In example 59 we ascend an Ab Dorian scale on the first chord, into a descending D minor triad over the Db7 chord—an upper structure triad that contains the b13, M3, and b9 intervals. We resolve to the P5 (Db) of the Gb6 by chromatic enclosure.

Ex. 60

Here is an example of playing all of Monk's changes, a la Johnny Griffin. The pitches on the A7 refer to the melody, then chromatically descend to the P5 of the D7. The D7-G7-C6 progression is treated with a chromatically descending two-note cell: A-B, Ab-Bb—then a resolution by leap to the P5 of the C6.

Ex. 61

Example 61 contains another unusual chord progression. The F7 doesn't resolve V-i to the Ebmin, although to my ears it makes sense to treat it as a super Locrian, or perhaps whole-tone, sound. On the Gb6 there is a scale fragment and a chromatic enclosure of the root of the F7, followed by a descending augmented sound on the F7. The P5 (Bb) resolution on the Ebmi7 is approached by half-step from below.

As I stated above, it is important to explore the nooks and crannies of Monk's harmony, especially on pieces like "Pannonica," "Ruby, My Dear," "Light Blue,"—tunes that aren't contrafacts of standards, but contain interesting, deceptive progressions as well as rapid cycles of dominant seventh chords. As always, the *Personalizing Jazz Vocabulary* method is a useful way to accomplish this goal.

MONK-TYPE CHANGES

Monk-Type Changes

(Mooney Improvisation)

61

CHAPTER 12

Shorter-Type Changes

The Wayne Shorter-esque harmony in this chapter is modal, somewhat along the lines of the Joe Henderson example in Chapter 6, and what ii-Vs there are, resolve deceptively.

Much of the language that I have written for this tune focuses on over-the-barline phrases that smooth out the deception of the harmonic movement. This is a technique I often use on this type of modern harmony. It can make harmonically awkward movements seem very natural. I think of it as the improvisational equivalent of contrary motion in counterpoint. Going against the grain, so to speak, can be aesthetically satisfying.

Ex. 62

The chord progression in measures 3-5 is Gmi7♭5-C7-BMaj7, minor ii-V that resolves deceptively: to BMaj7 instead of Fmin. In this example, I have treated the C7 as an augmented sound, with pitches taken mostly from the super Locrian scale. **The resolution note, the M7 A♯ of the BMaj7 chord, also functions enharmonically as the ♭7 (B♭) of the C7—a *negative guide tone*. This creates an over-the-barline effect as the C7 flows smoothly into the BMaj7 without the need for an emphatic resolution.**

Ex. 63

Measures 9-12 of this progression contain a whimsical series of chords—colors really: EMaj7-A7sus-A♭7♯11-G♭7sus. As with example 62, this line attempts to smooth the unusual transition from the A Mixolydian sound of the A7sus to the E♭ melodic minor sound of the A♭7♯11, two scales that only have D and F♯ pitches in common.

Ex. 64

In example 64, an A super Locrian scale descends stepwise from C natural. There is only one skip, F down to C♯, and the line resolves to A♭6 with a chromatic toggle between C and B natural. This M3 (C) on the A♭6 chord has already been heard twice over the A7; its familiarity helps to smooth out the unusual resolution.

Ex. 65

Example 65 contains a longer line than usual. In this case, I'm attempting to connect three separate, non-functional sounds by way of negative guide tones. These negative guide tones are G natural on the B♭mi7 and E♭7♯11, and G♯ on the AMaj7. One could also analyze the material over the B♭mi7 chord as coming from the C minor pentatonic scale, while the AMaj7 material hails from C♯ minor pentatonic. **The line ascends through these pentatonic scales, even as the bass notes of the chords descend, creating contrary motion.**

Ex. 66

In this example, I have used classic jazz chromaticism over the highly modern harmony. The resolution is by half step, from the P5 (D♭) of the G♭7sus to the ♭7 (D) of the E7sus.

The language that I write for students to improvise around on modern, modal progressions like this—as well as on progressions that jump around to distant key centers, like Coltrane changes—is constructed to smooth out the deceptive, disjointed chord movement, and to cut against the grain and provide a contrast: simplicity against complexity. There is a difference, in my mind, between resolutions that seek to simplify a progression like this chapter's EMaj7-A7sus-A♭7♯11-G♭7sus and the *classic jazz language* that seeks to add dissonance and complexity to a common, functional ii-V-I or cycle of dominants.

The *Personalizing Jazz Vocabulary* method of improvising into and out of the examples while playing the examples themselves exactly as written remains the same, even as the language and the aesthetic goal of that language shift.

*Page left blank to avoid
awkward page turns.*

SHORTER-TYPE CHANGES

Shorter-Type Changes

(Mooney Improvisation)

CHAPTER 13

And Then?

The *Personalizing Jazz Vocabulary* method has served me and my students well in incorporating classic jazz vocabulary into our inherently original improvising voices. But this method is only a preliminary step in the ultimate quest of the jazz musician: to develop a unique, identifiable sound.

There are seeming contradictions at work here, as is often the case when one cracks open the bones of complex, important questions to get at the marrow. Why is it necessary or desirable to assimilate and personalize the jazz language—which is after all, a collection of tropes and licks that is by definition *un*original—if the ultimate goal of the improvising jazz musician is *uniqueness?*

Any honest answer would have to begin with; "It isn't necessary at all." Our uniqueness and originality are already there; they are inherent. And yet, as musicians (and as human beings in a larger sense), we are going to assimilate and be shaped by what we hear, whether it's the jazz tradition, or Balinese Gamelan music, or punk rock, or what have you.

Any style of music has a history, and a collection of tropes and customs and recognized practices that define it as itself, and not some other style. Even within jazz there are many traditions, and this *classic jazz vocabulary*—which I have defined largely by giving examples rather than taking an historiographical approach—is often contrasted by students with free jazz or "time, no changes," or the current universe of post-modern and deconstructionist jazz. But all of these styles, which we classify as "jazz" due to the common thread of improvisation—have their own tropes, practices, and yes, even licks.

My point is, you can't avoid the issue of integrating and personalizing some universe of musical language into your own inherent improvising voice. You can only choose which series of tropes and practices you want to integrate. In some sense, this is what developing a *unique sound* really entails. Perhaps another book could describe a method to accomplish this.

And yet, who doesn't like to play "name that influence" when listening to someone take a solo? As we get deeper into the jazz tradition, and assimilate more language, it becomes possible to identify the source of almost everything that everyone plays, much as when you hear someone from your culture speak, you can identify what television shows, pop songs or geographic region influenced their collection of expressions.

There is something transcendent that has to happen, I suppose, for someone to sound like *themself* rather than a collection of other people. Or perhaps we just decide as a community that so and so is original, as back in middle school we agreed who was hot and who was not.

I have constructed my own improvising voice out of a collection of classic jazz and modern jazz tropes that appealed to my sense of aesthetic *rightness*, but I suspect I would lose myself irrevocably if I tried to break down where that rightness comes from.

Then again, the jazz tradition is important to me. I love the sound of classic jazz, and I know how difficult it is to "master"—if such a thing were possible. So I have made it my life's work to continue that tradition and pass it on to students.

Hence this book, which describes my methods, my brand of theoretical analysis, and my aesthetic choices.

Hopefully it can be of some assistance to students who have experienced a disconnect such as the one described in Chapter 1, which is perhaps a symptom of a larger disconnect between being an individual improvising musician, while also being part of a collection of improvising musician communities.